WHAT IS AN ECLIPSE?

BY ISAAC ASIMOV

Gareth Stevens Children's Books

MILWAUKEE

For a free color catalog describing Gareth Stevens' list of high-quality children's books, call 1-800-341-3569 (USA) or 1-800-461-9120 (Canada).

Library of Congress Cataloging-in-Publication Data

Asimov, Isaac, 1920-
    What is an eclipse? / by Isaac Asimov. — A Gareth Stevens Children's Books ed.
        p.   cm. — (Ask Isaac Asimov)
    Includes bibliographical references and index.
    Summary: A step-by-step description of how an eclipse occurs and the differences
between a lunar and a solar eclipse.
    ISBN 0-8368-0440-6
    1. Eclipses—Juvenile literature. [1. Eclipses.] I. Title. II. Series: Asimov, Isaac, 1920-
Ask Isaac Asimov.
QB175.A85 1991
523.7'8—dc20   90-26062

A Gareth Stevens Children's Books edition

Edited, designed, and produced by
Gareth Stevens Children's Books
1555 North RiverCenter Drive, Suite 201
Milwaukee, Wisconsin 53212, USA

Picture Credits
pp. 2-3, National Optical Astronomy Observatories; pp. 4-5, courtesy of NASA; p. 5 (inset), Keith Ward; pp. 6-7, E. W. Perry/Third Coast, © 1987; p. 6 (inset), Gareth Stevens, Inc.; pp. 8-11, Pat Rawlings; pp. 12-13, courtesy of NASA; pp. 14-15, Pat Rawlings; p. 16, © George East; p. 17, Craig Calsbeck; p. 18, Gareth Stevens, Inc.; p. 19, © Richard Baum; pp. 20-24, courtesy of NASA

Cover photograph, courtesy of NASA: Total eclipse of the Sun, taken at Miahuatlan, Mexico, on March 7, 1970. Scientists from fourteen different nations traveled to Mexico to observe this solar eclipse.

Series editor: Elizabeth Kaplan
Editor: Patricia Lantier-Sampon
Series designer: Sabine Huschke
Picture researcher: Daniel Helminak
Picture research assistant: Diane Laska
Consulting editors: Matthew Groshek and John D. Rateliff

Printed in MEXICO

1 2 3 4 5 6 7 8 9 97 96 95 94 93 92 91

Contents

Words that appear in the glossary are printed in **boldface** type the first time they occur in the text.

A World of Questions

Our world is full of strange and beautiful things. For instance, from time to time, a dark shadow crosses the face of the Sun or the Moon. People used to think a dragon was gobbling up the Sun or the Moon. They would bang on pots and pans to scare away the dragon and bring back the light.

Today we know that such changes in the appearance of the Sun or the Moon are not caused by dragons but by **eclipses**. What is an eclipse? Let's find out.

Hide and Seek

An eclipse occurs whenever one thing moves in front of another and hides it. The Sun, the Moon, even stars, can be eclipsed. A cloud can pass in front of the Sun or Moon and hide it. That's a kind of eclipse. The Sun or Moon can pass behind a tall building. That's a kind of eclipse, too.

If you put your hand up in front of your eyes to shield them from the Sun, your hand is eclipsing the Sun. These are only a few examples of eclipses.

Eclipsing the Sun

When the Moon moves in front of the Sun, a **solar eclipse** occurs. During a solar eclipse, the Moon slowly passes in front of the Sun, until the Sun is almost completely hidden. Then, the Sun looks like a black circle surrounded by a halo of reddish light. The halo is really the Sun's **atmosphere** flaring around the rim of the darkened Sun.

As the Moon moves past the face of the Sun, the Sun shines again. Solar eclipses only occur when the Earth, the Moon, and the Sun all line up in a straight line.

8

Sun

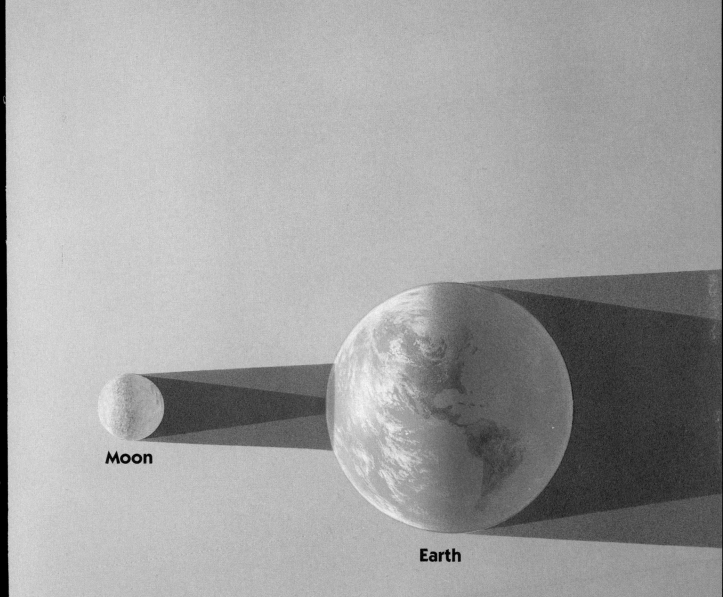

Moon

Earth

Moon Shadows

During a solar eclipse, the Moon casts its shadow on Earth. This picture shows how this shadow might look from the Moon.

The Moon's shadow has two parts: a small dark part at the center of the shadow, called the **umbra**, and a larger, lighter part surrounding the umbra, called the **penumbra**. From Earth, you will see a solar eclipse if you are in either the umbra or the penumbra of the Moon's shadow.

Whole or Part?

If you are in the Moon's umbra, you will see a **total eclipse** of the Sun. But if you are in the penumbra, you will see only a **partial eclipse**. In a total eclipse, the Moon completely covers the Sun. In a partial eclipse, the Moon hides part of the Sun. This makes the Sun look as if a notch has been punched out of its edge, as shown above.

Partial solar eclipses are more common than total eclipses. On the average, a total solar eclipse will occur at a given spot on Earth only once every 350 years!

Eclipsing the Moon

When Earth moves directly between the Sun and the Moon, a **lunar eclipse** occurs. During a lunar eclipse, Earth's shadow travels across the face of the Moon. The shadow blocks out the moonlight. But the Moon does not turn completely black. Sunlight passing through Earth's atmosphere bounces off the face of the Moon. This light gives the eclipsed Moon an eerie reddish orange color. Unlike a solar eclipse, a lunar eclipse can be seen from every place on Earth where the Moon is visible.

14

Sun

Earth

Moon

In and Out of the Umbra

A total lunar eclipse occurs when the umbra of Earth's shadow covers the Moon entirely. During the middle of a total lunar eclipse, the entire surface of the Moon darkens for an hour or two.

When only part of the umbra passes over the face of the Moon, we have a partial lunar eclipse. During the middle of a partial lunar eclipse, the Moon looks as if a chunk has been taken out of it.

Transits and Occultations

We can see eclipses with other planets and stars. Mercury and Venus sometimes pass in front of the Sun. We call this event a **transit**. During a transit, Mercury and Venus look like tiny dots moving across the Sun's face. The pictures on these pages show Mercury passing in front of the Sun during a transit.

During an **occultation**, a **heavenly body** blocks the light from a star. Occultations often happen with double stars, which circle each other in close orbit. Sometimes one of the two stars passes in front of the other, blocking our view of the more distant star. The closer star occults, or hides, the other star.

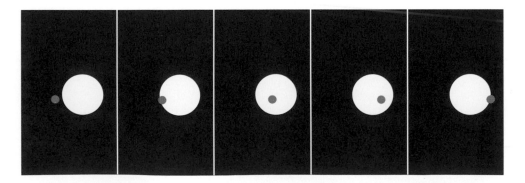

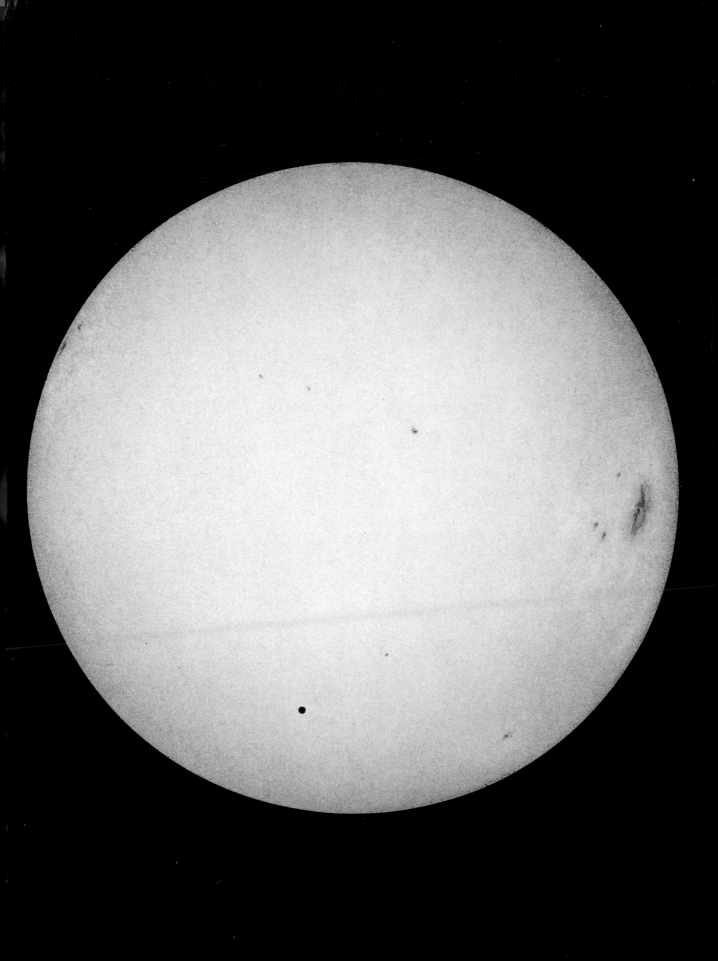

To See or Not to See

You need a telescope to get a good view of transits and occultations. But for a lunar eclipse, you can just watch as the Moon slowly turns reddish orange.

Solar eclipses, however, are dangerous to watch unless you take special precautions. The Sun's burning rays can damage your eyes. To watch a solar eclipse, poke a small hole in a piece of cardboard and hold the cardboard parallel to the ground. The hole will make an image of the Sun that you can project onto a smooth, light-colored surface. Look down at the image and watch how it changes shape as the eclipse progresses.

WARNING:

NEVER LOOK DIRECTLY AT THE SUN. NEVER LOOK AT THE SUN THROUGH A TELESCOPE OR BINOCULARS.

An Unearthly Beauty

Which do you think would be more beautiful, a solar eclipse or a lunar eclipse? Some people think that the Sun's dramatic darkening makes a solar eclipse very exciting. Other people say that the strange orange glow of the eclipsed Moon makes a lunar eclipse more haunting than the disappearing Sun. Most people agree that eclipses are among the most awe-inspiring events that we can witness in the heavens.

More Books to Read

The Earth's Moon by Isaac Asimov (Gareth Stevens)
Eclipse: Darkness in Daytime by Donald Crews (Harper & Row
    Junior Books)
The Sun by Isaac Asimov (Gareth Stevens)

Places to Write

Here are some places you can write to for more information about
eclipses, transits, and occultations. Be sure to tell them exactly
what you want to know about. Give them your full name and
address so that they can write back to you.

National Space Society
600 Maryland Avenue SW
Washington, D.C. 20024

Stardate
McDonald Observatory
Austin, Texas 78712

Space Communications Branch
Ministry of State for Science
    and Technology
240 Sparks Street
C. D. Howe Building
Ottawa, Ontario K1A 1A1

Glossary

atmosphere (AT-muhs-fear): the gases that surround a planet, star,
    or moon.

eclipse (ee-KLIPS): an event that involves the passage of an object
    in front of a heavenly body, so that light from that body is
    blocked for a time.

heavenly body: any star, planet, moon, or other natural object that
    is found in space.

lunar eclipse: an eclipse that occurs when the Earth's shadow passes over the face of the Moon; during this time, Earth, the Moon, and the Sun all align in a straight line.

occultation (ah-kuhl-TAY-shun): an event that occurs when a heavenly body blocks the light from a star.

partial eclipse: an eclipse in which the face of a heavenly body is only partly blocked at most.

penumbra (peh-NUM-bruh): the light outer part of a shadow.

solar eclipse: an eclipse that occurs when the Moon passes between Earth and the Sun; during this time, Earth, the Moon, and the Sun all align in a straight line.

total eclipse: an eclipse in which the face of a heavenly body is completely blocked during for a time.

transit (TRANN-ziht): an event during which Mercury or Venus passes in front of the Sun as viewed from Earth.

umbra (UHM-bruh): the dark central part of a shadow.

Index